ABOUT THE AUTHOR

Casey Bailey is a writer, poet, spoken word performer, rapper
and secondary school senior leader from Birmingham, with a
Masters in Education pulling together his passion for the
development of people and academia. He provides social
commentary and analysis through his poetry, lyrics and articles.

Casey is most comfortable when he is consciously expressing his
thoughts and feelings, with the hope that they will go on to have
an impact on the thoughts and feelings of others.

Casey released the short poetry collection *Waiting At Bloomsbury
Park* with Big White Shed in 2017.

Twitter: @MrCaseyBailey
www.baileysrapandpoetry.com
www.facebook.com/baileysrapandpoetry
www.soundcloud.com/baileys-rap-and-poetry

Casey Bailey
Adjusted

VERVE
POETRY PRESS

BIRMINGHAM

PUBLISHED BY VERVE POETRY PRESS
Birmingham, West Midlands, UK
www.vervepoetrypress.com
mail@vervepoetrypress.com

FIRST PUBLISHED APR 2018

Printed and bound in the UK
by TJ International, Padstow

ISBN: 978-1-912565-02-3

This book is dedicated to Earl Bailey, the greatest man I've ever known

and

Xander Jay Bailey, the boy who I hope will surpass him.

CONTENTS

Adjusted

Lost
&
Found

Lost In Foundness

I am found,
in an independent coffee shop
discussing the Arab-Israeli conflict
with a homeless woman
I just met outside.
She is not going to let
the caramel macchiato
that I have just bought her
sway her to agree with me.

I am growing out of
wearied ideologies
that I never really believed,
growing into fresh spaces
I've always belonged in.
I am one more paradox
in a world of inconsistencies.

I am a teacher in a school
that would have kicked
me out as a pupil.
I am trapped between
ghetto kids need more to do
and
ghetto kids need to do more.

A dove brandishing
an olive branch like a knife,
I have transitioned

from fighting for a piece
to petitioning for peace
so quickly that I am
equipped for both,
prepared for neither.

The bull made from china,
I dare not move, knowing
I am more likely to break

myself than anything else.
In this world of red rags
I am a time bomb with a
broken clock.
Watch me,
but don't look at me
like you know me.

I am lost;
unsure of who
or where I am
but I know where
I belong now.

We Drink For Them

We stand heads bowed on a street corner
that he used to stand on, his head up, shoulders back.
A passer-by might think that we're praying.
We don't pray.

I grab the back of your neck and clutch it like you were him,
you hold me like you recognise that I'm not.
My dry palms, heavy on your sweat-wet skin,
my eye contact, exposes me to an agony
in your eyes that I'm petrified to share.

We're passing a bottle of Steamers around, no cups,
chests getting warmer as our hearts grow colder.
Alcohol has always been medicine here, never a cure.
Two empty bottles on the floor, as we dive again
the bottle is faster, we swim deeper.

You pour a little to the ground *dead homies gotta drink.*
We manage a *mmmmm*, keep tipping.
Tip it for the boy raised in a grim cul-de-sac.
Tip it for the boy in the middle of a ghetto, crumbling.
Tip it for the boy who lost his dad to crime
and lost his life to criminals.
Tip it.
There are only so many ways you can say dead end
before it becomes a self-fulfilling prophecy.

Now we listen as you share your philosophy,
everybody has to die, nobody likes it
but either way we all have to live with it
till we don't.
You simplify complex pain,
bridging deep wounds with shallow words.
We accept it, he was your brother.

As the bottle speeds up
each new drinker calls a name
putting life back into our dead friends.

We drink for them
It's all we've got.

The Last Time I Cried

I caught my tears in my hands
like I was counting them.
Why am I catching my tears?
I will not catch the smell of her cooking
dancing through the house, stew chicken
on a Sunday with a small pot of plain rice
because I don't like the peas.
I grasp for the magnificence of her smile,
too broad to hold, and the tapping rhythm
of her patios, melodic and captivating.

I raised these hands to wipe these eyes;
removing nothing.
New tears washed away with old tears
as newer tears forced the cycle to continue.

I stared from a window
I can't remember looking from
out onto a view that I recognised
in an instant. She used to hold me here.
She'd sing me old school RnB songs here
because lullabies are boring
and I don't understand the words anyway.

Now I stare, singing Toni Braxton
Another Sad Love Song finally realising
how sad it is, how easily music
that raised us can annihilate our souls.

Now I wrestle to keep tears in.
I am comfortable with crying,
I can't cry every time I think of her.
My hands do not have the space
to hold that flood,
my brain does not have the capacity
to calculate those tears.
So, I don't cry,
I just think about the last time I did.

Crack In The Pavement

I still remember the first time
I saw a crackhead holding a crack pipe,
12 years old, totally misunderstanding
the relationship of owner and owned.

These days I have lost count
of the amount of crack pipes
I have seen gripping people.
I have learned not to measure people
by the mistakes that they make.

When I was 13 I learnt that pressure bursts pipes,
when I was 14 I learnt that pressure breaks people,
when I was 15 I learnt that sometimes broken people
find themselves in broken pipes,
willing to inhale anything that cuts
the taste of pressurised air.

Have you ever seen the hollow,
carved out carcasses of your dreams?
Ever been stuck in a trench
that is deeper than despair
and narrower than the line
between smiling and showing
your teeth because it hurts less
than discussing your pain?
If not,
do not tell me what you
would never do.

Pointing the finger is physically
the closest thing to extending a hand
but always done by those who, morally,
couldn't be further away if they tried.

Spirit

There's a 3/4 full bottle of Courvoisier behind your back.
When you see that it's me coming up your stairs
the sigh of relief is audible, like the 66 bus hydraulics,
1/2 the tension in your shoulders rushed from your body
like we used to rush from that bus when it stopped at Star City.
We. You, me and him.

You pull the Courvoisier bottle out now, I look at you,
we never really know what to say at times like this,
where people say nothing, or say something stupid
and I never know what's worst, but I never get it right.

You were hiding that painkiller, but not from me,
so as I sit down you screw the lid off and look at me;
I can't do this shit sober Case, no way I can't do it. Big swig.
I reach for the bottle and you smile, not happy or sad,
just a smile of unity, *I'm with you, you're with me.*

I feel my cheeks water as the bottle rises, nostrils widen,
I match your swig and follow it with a small one
as the walls of my throat become a chimney breathing
back the heat of the fire I just started in my stomach.

There are 5 cars and about 15 people waiting outside
your house for us to surface, there is a body in a church
that we are not ready for but just like them he won't wait
forever so it's now or never *let's do this bro, let's go.*

There's 1/2 a bottle of Courvoisier in your room
and no tension in your shoulders as we free ourselves.
Today we carry his coffin, tomorrow we carry his spirit.

Best

You wore personality
like a mobile phone case
so even when the world
struck you it couldn't
damage you.

When I talk about you
I say *best friend*
never just *friend*.
I don't know if that
is to ensure that you
know what you mean to me,
or so they know
how much I am hurting.

You were
already broken,
brain exhausted
from fabricating demons
and fighting them off.

When I wake from
dreaming about you,
I clamp my eyes
shut, desperate
not to lose you
again.

The Diary Entry Before Your Suicide Note

Dear Diary,

I tried to do it today, I couldn't.
I will do it tomorrow, I have to.

If I don't stand up for me
nobody will, and even if I do
they won't.
I can't wait for a hero
to save me,
I've got to save myself.
I feel like it's now or never
and I never want to feel
like now again.

I can't hear about the difference
between sticks and stones
and words again,
when physical pain
is the only distraction
that I have from the real hurt
that I feel.

I will do it tomorrow, I have to
and the next time I write in this book
it won't be to say he's done it again.
If he does, I probably won't feel like writing.

I Know How I'm Supposed To Feel

I know how I'm supposed to feel.
I know the ground doesn't swallow people,
I know that walls don't move
to close in on me.
Walls don't move.
Collars on t-shirts don't tighten.
I know this,
but this isn't all I know.

I have sat on the bottom of the ocean,
I have drowned with the weight
of the sea on top of me,
I have opened my eyes to find an exam hall.

Bright sun doesn't brighten dark days.
Wise words can't calm raging waters,
raging waters of a beating heart
that shake and break minds that were once steady.

I know how I'm supposed to feel.
I know I've never had surgery on my chest.
So why have I felt hands
creeping inside my rib cage?
Why have I felt fists
squeezing my lungs, thumping my heart,
blocking my throat so I can't breathe,
can't speak, can't scream for help?

I need help.

I know how I'm supposed to feel,
I know, I know, I know.

But I don't
feel like that.

I feel pressure
to not put pressure on myself,
I feel anxious about anxiety,
I feel blood pausing
in my veins. Rusting.

People tell me to relax,
seriously.
Like I would be here
if I could relax on demand.

I know this isn't logical,
know I don't really have a reason
to be stressed
and there is nothing
more stressful than knowing that.

I know how I'm supposed to feel.
But I don't know what that feels like.

Ignorance Ignored

I tell him that his words can't affect me,
he repeats his slur. I laugh,
reminding myself that the basis of the word
ignorance is the word ignore.

I congratulate him on his persistence,
apologise for not reciprocating
in an appropriate manner. How
very unexpected of me, how rude.

I understand what he does. He has his
finger on a trigger and he's squeezing.
It is only in recent years
I have come to understand what he doesn't;
I am not a gun or the savage that he
believed me to be. I never was.

When he asks me where I lost my chains
I laugh, tell him I left them with my
puppet strings, somewhere near his
control over me, tell him if he finds them
he can have them. It's unfair of me,
I know. Just like I know this boy will
never find those chains, or that control.

I can be so mean sometimes.

Last Drink

I hope that's her last drink
they tell each other;
they judge the woman,
with the drinking problem,
with the kids at home,
with no control or shame.
How can she be here now?
I feel sorry for the kids.

But the kids only feel sorry
when she stops drinking
and comes home to them,
with the drinking problem,
with no control or shame.
Everybody wants a mother
but nobody wants this one.
They hope it's not her last drink.

Mutual

I am 15 seconds into this YouTube video.
The Syrian boy who looks no more than 15
says the same thing for the third time,

Please do not think us to be savages

At least this is what the subtitles say.

This time he elaborates beyond the statement:

Please do not think us to be savages,
we cry for our dead like you cry for yours,
parents hug children, children hug tighter.
We do not wish this for you any more
than we have wished it for ourselves, I promise.

Please do not think us to be savages,
do not think that the people who hurt you
are people who represent us, they are not.
We do not smile for your pain, some will,
but not us, we take no joy in your death.

Please do not think us to be savages,
we have lost count of those we have lost
but we have not lost our faith in our god,
not lost the love that makes our hearts warm,
not lost hope, hope for us, hope for everyone.

When the video stops, I allow myself to breath,
I allow myself to cry tears, tears of pain,
tears of grief, tears of blood, tears of shame.

I want to record him a video in response,
tell him he could communicate with me
without any need for subtitles or translations,
tell him that I understood his tortured plea
before he took the time to share it with me.

I want to record him a video in response
but I do not want to steal his words from him
and I feel the way he feels, except I feel
incapable of matching the eloquence of his emotion.

I click on the comments symbol and I type,

The feeling is mutual.

Glass Heart

I will keep providing you
with opportunities to break me.
I don't have to,

I could link the bond
of this relationship
to my trust,
tell you that if you break one
you break both.

I won't do that,

I will hand you this glass heart
knowing that you haven't been exposed
to this level of fragility before.
Conscious that you may fumble it,
I will hand it to you.

If you break it, we will fix it,
I will hand it to you again
and again, I will learn to love
the reflection of you in the seams
of the cracks

and you will learn
the beautiful dangers
of trust.

I will hand you the patched-up pieces
of my heart hoping
it will fix yours
and you will let somebody hold it
again.

Him. Her.. You…

.

I buried my heart
six feet under
heavy dirt
and dusty memories.

. .

When I found it
again, I cremated
it, with burning tears
and searing flames
of grief.

. . .

When you arrived
I knew my heart
was back, my tired,
blistered feet could rest.
I settled down.
I was ready
to stop travelling.

Rise And Fall

I never understood
why the sun fell
until I met her;

now I, like the sun,
fall for her every night
and rise for her
every morning.

Step Step

I am not a dancer,
but don't tell that to my feet
when the city plays this beat
and the concrete becomes
a dance floor to navigate.

It was in a garage rave at 17
that I first realised
you can't just walk
across a dance floor,
you have to blend, move,
move with them to move through them.

This is one of the few rules
that I never break. Ever.

From the train at Grand Central
to Yo Sushi at Selfridges
is not a walk, but a waltz.

Eyes up for the skyscrapers
letting pockets of sunshine through.
Step step.
Twist left so the young couple don't
have to release each other's hands.
Step step.
Spot the homeless man from 100 yards,
sort the coins before I get there.
Step step.

He has seen this city at its coldest
and knows this song never ends.
Step step.

Never miss a beat, always in time.
Shoulders brush, bags clash,
step back to let somebody else
pass but never stop.
Like joggers, waiting for green men
to tell them to cross the road;
feet still drumming at the same tempo.

I am gliding through Brum,
a busker plays guitar, singing,
I just wanna live, don't really care
about the things that they say, don't
really care about what happens to me.

At the same time a girl, no older than 10
races downhill along the wall of the
Floozi In The Jacuzzi fountain,
head forwards, arms backward,
as if dipping for a gold medal.

The image of her and sound of his lyrics
plait together like her swinging pigtails.

Mini motion picture.

I hear him, I see her,
I feel all of it!

Twist right, don't knock her coffee,
clutch slightly tighter to mine.
Step step.
Apologise to the homeless woman,
knowing I gave that change already.
Step step.
Tell her she is not a 'bother' at all,
wish her a good day in return.
Step step.
Check my pockets as I meander away;
we both look for hope we've lost.
Step step.

It was at a funeral at 19,
when I first came to understand,
you can't treat people
like they are any more
or any less than human.

This is one of the few rules
that I never break. Ever.

Head up, rhythm steady,
The dance floor remains packed,
this DJ takes no requests.
We move, all together all apart.

I am not dancer
but this city plays a song
that my heart can't deny
and my feet can't disregard.

Two Blue Lines

On May 14th 2017 I became father to Xander Jay Bailey. The poems in this section reflect upon the journey that we have been on.

Two Blue Lines

Having said goodbye
to my mother this year,
we know that this
was not the only loss
we suffered,
we have seen two blue lines fade
faster than they could ever appear.

We became the parents
of numbness
with no clue what to feed it
or dress it in, no support groups
to attend, just solitude
even when together, solitude
with no smiles or milestones
to keep us going just a numbness
that was growing like a child should.
would we grieve
forever.

We cry over two new blue lines
now, I smile,
not because of how I feel
but because of how you need
me to feel.

I cannot be the man who drowns
on the day that you need
me to be the man he keeps you afloat.

Thumping

I heard my baby's heartbeat.
My wife lay on a little hospital bed,
the nurse with her thick Black
Country accent spoke,
Arrr that's beautiful that aye it?

I heard my baby's heart beat;
horses thumping on Roman streets,
chariots drawn to Rome, I heard
the prince or princess of my empire.

I heard my baby's heartbeat,
perfect rhythm, definitely
inherited from me, I have
seen Mom dance and I hope
that this baby never has to.

I felt my heart beat.
Supposed to pump blood
around my body, but today
pumping water to my eyes,
I could give birth to tears
looking into the eyes of my wife
who will soon give birth to a life.

The child will be ours,
but the life will be yours.

I heard your heart beat today.

Nail Marks

He was born an hour ago,
he's sleeping and you're sleeping
whilst I examine these nail marks.

Red tracks.
Soviet flag red,
blood pressing the underside of skin
threatening to break through
like you were threatening to last night.

Tracks.
Lorry tyres pressing on fresh snow,
you left tracks.
Pressure applied,
pain passed person to person
leaving inscriptions.

The marks will fade.
The landing of fresh snow
or the blazing sun will erase them
but they will never take the journey away,
never change the destination.

I examine these nail marks,
clear in the conviction
that you could have butchered my hands
and I'd still be overjoyed right now.

Best Work

I am making the pledge to myself
that I made when I was eight years old,
holding an actual pen
with real ink
that can't be rubbed out.

I have drafted and redrafted this,
written it out in pencil
using a dictionary for spellings,
I have erased letters, words, paragraphs,
to turn this into something worth showing.

I have shown it to those who know better,
asked for advice
and ignored a lot of it,
this is mine and I know
what I want it to be like.
Miss doesn't like how I structure things,
Daniel thinks I write I too much,
it's not their work though, is it?

Now I cradle you,
afraid of what these hands could do.
I am an eight-year-old,
clumsily clutching a pen
on assessment day,
ready to do my best work.
I know exactly what I want to do,
but it only takes one mistake.

I make the same pledge to myself
That I made when I was eight years old.
I'm gonna take my time,
I'm gonna get this right.

Beautiful Disasters

I have mastered the art of finding humour in my failure.
I have come to know we all have gifts,
that we all have limitations,
and some of us get it wrong more
spectacularly than others.

As a footballer, I have scored more goals
against my goal keeper than against theirs,
some of those goals were stunning.
Beautiful disasters, fluorescent volcanic eruptions,
tsunamis that wave their majesty at the world.
Beautiful disasters.

Today I experienced my most beautiful disaster,
my most hilarious act of uselessness yet.
As a man cradling your baby,
physically supporting a universe with just your arms,
there is nothing more magically futile
than watching as he attempts to suckle
from your milk-less chest.

Nothing more magically useless,
nothing more perfectly imperfect,
no disaster more beautiful than us.

In this moment
there is nothing more amazing than him,
nothing more useless than me.

Apples and Trees

When the corners
of your mouth drop,
my heart plummets
fruitlessly to catch them,

I visualise apples
and trees.
I consider of landings.

I pray we will always
be as close as we are now,
your head on my chest
your heart in my mind.

When all else fails
I raise you towards
the lights on the ceiling
you are distracted,
you are calmed.

I tell myself
if ever I can't retrieve
you from the darkness
I will bring the light
to you.

Search History

Pregnancy after miscarriage

Best vitamins for pregnant women to take

Discount price pregnancy vitamins

Baby names

Funny celebrity baby names

What is Hypno-birthing

Baby names

Middle names

How to start labour naturally

Induced labour

Healing after a caesarean section

Baby blues

Is it dangerous to smile all day?

I Want My Mom

I haven't felt like this for decades.
I hold the desperation of a toddler
deep in my chest today.
I want my mom.

I know she can't come,
know she would
if she could.

I want my mom
for the times when we cry
about your crying,
ready to compete
with a 5 week old
about who is more exhausted,

for the times when you will cry,
when people let you down,
when shooting stars
turn out to be crashing planes
and you've wasted a wish,

for the times you are David
staring at Goliath
with no sling to hold.
She would arm you.
I never walked into battle unarmed.

For the times when your heart implodes,
when you are tired and flat,
when your tyre is flat.
She would inflate you,
pumping compressed love
until your chest was just above
its recommended pressure.

I haven't felt like this for decades.
I hold the desperation of a toddler
deep in my chest today.
I want my mom
for my son.

Pre-empted

I wish I could have pre-empted you,
if I did I would have pre-emptied me.

I knew that you were coming,
but to know of your imminence,
isn't to know of your eminence.

To know that you would arrive,
is not knowledge of your impact,
I'm surprised I am intact, you hit hard.

I am a suitcase in a blazing desert,
holding jeans instead of shorts,
mislead by reports of a storm coming.

I am wasting space holding anything
that isn't you, or for you, or of you,
I'm wasting space, I was not ready.

I am a vegan's fridge stuffed with meat
that no one will eat, nobody wants that,
you are tofu and spinach and goodness.

I am wasting time thinking about how
I make space, when I should have already,
I should have been ready, I couldn't have.

I knew what I was, but didn't know you yet,
knew I was a pen, never knew you were ink,
knew I was a chest, now my hearts here.

To know that you would arrive
is not knowledge of your impact,
I'm surprised I am intact, you hit hard.

I knew that you were coming,
but to know of your imminence,
isn't to know of your eminence.

I wish I could have pre-empted you,
If I did I would have pre-emptied me.

See Saw

Since you've been here, the days have become a see saw,
my sleep pattern and your sleep pattern on opposite ends.
Every time I try to get down, you think it's time to get up.

I
     get
         down,
              you get up,
I get down,
       you
          get
            up,

The days are broken, sleep is a stranger,
your overworked vocal chords are as strained as I am,
My ear drums are more tender than you.

You
     get
         down,
             I get up,
You get down,
       I
         get
           up,

You wake sending screams like distress signals,
I hold you; the recognition in your eyes
calms you and melts me; we wake, we sleep
restart and repeat. We swing

up   down,

            and

backwards   forwards.

            and

As long as we share this, I know I'll appreciate it.
For once in my life, the fact that I can't get no sleep,
doesn't leave me faithless, I am faithful and grateful.

Questions

It's June 13th 2017
tomorrow is my Dad's birthday
today you are 4 weeks old.
I reflect on the lessons
he taught me,
consider how I'll share them,
do I need to share them?
Will you need to hear
about oppression and inequality?
Will it help you?

I am fighting to build
you a future that rises above
the issues of my childhood.
I don't know if you'll need
to appreciate the struggles
that I have seen. Why show
you then? Why protect you
from suffering just to introduce
you to it anyway? Do you need
to know? Do I need to tell you?

Is it possible to eradicate
the inequalities of society?
Is it possible to make them
irrelevant?

In 12 hours a fire will start
at Grenfell tower.
In 12 hours a flame
and combustible cladding
will answer my questions.

Footprints

There are one set of footprints
pressed decisively into this sand.

I carry you down a path
that you did not select for yourself,
knowing you may, one day,
deviate from it.

I tread these footsteps weightily
and purposefully.
I will never force you to follow,
but I will guarantee that you can see them,
just in case.

It is my job to build you a compass,
it will be your job to choose your direction.

Midnight Theory

On July 20th 2016 my mother passed away after a battle with lung cancer. On July 20th 2017 Chester Bennington, the lead singer of my favourite band Linkin' Park, took his own life. I grew up as a Linkin' Park fan, in an area where most people wouldn't listen to their style of music. When I told my mom I liked their Hybrid Theory album and that no one would understand that, she told me to be who I was, love what I loved and never change either for others. The poems in this section find their basis in the lyrics of my favourite Linkin' Park songs and explore mental health, suicide, loss and darkness.

In The End

I
Appreciate moments in the middle of madness,
It's ok to feel helpless when the rain seems to fall
inside your umbrella, helpless like parentless children
or childless parents who end stories in the middle
and prayers at the start, unable to trust
the ears of listeners or the ears of God.

I have tried to forget. On the darkest nights
of my existence, I have tried to convince
myself that it was only you who lay helpless,
no pain tore at my torso, the swelling pressure
in my tear ducts couldn't burst river banks,
earth blistering tears, falling like crushed people
do after realising the dangers of trust.

II
How many land mines do you have to step
on, to never trust the ground again?
How many Linkin' Park songs have I tried
listening to thinking they were safe now?
Mom's first anniversary, Chester Bennington
ended his life, the knife in my gut twists again.

I feel pressure to keep this news to myself,
put my phone down because I can't trust
myself not to say this out loud, Chester Bennington
is dead. They don't want to hear this now.

III
You are feeble, falling down, falling apart,
falling victim to the cold trapped beneath your ribs.
You keep everything inside, knowing how helpless
you were the last time you let any of it out, the last time
you chose trust over safety, or trust because it felt safe.

Anybody who has tried to find themselves in the strength
of another learned it is better falling for your own beliefs.
When you feel helpless remember, even she was in the end.

Multiple Choice

Find a new place to hang this noose.
Stop killing those who already killed themselves
like they haven't suffered enough already,
carried enough already,
died enough already.

To label somebody a coward
when they are no longer here
to represent themselves,
has to be the worst cocktail
of cowardice and hypocrisy
I have tasted.

Maybe he did it because he
had lost all hope in this life.
Maybe she did it because her only hope
was that another life would follow.
I always thought the most difficult
multiple choice questions
are the ones where you feel like all
of the answers could be right.

Gravity is pulling us all down
just because bricks fall faster
than feathers,
doesn't mean they're weaker,
they just carry more weight.

A man who looked young
but aged, with a face
like distressed furniture,
told me that the greatest
misconception about suicidal people,
is the thought that they want to die.
Nobody desires death,
the issue is, that not everybody
wants to live, either.

The most difficult multiple choice questions
are not the ones where you feel like all
of the answers could be right.
The most difficult multiple choice questions
are the ones where you feel like none
of the answers can be right,
but you must choose one anyway.

I Have

I have sat
head slumped
until my neck aches.
Nothing sits heavier
than weightlessness
on the shoulders of those
who only ever wanted
to hold weight.
I have washed my blood
from my hands,
thanking all the things
I don't believe in
that it wasn't yours. Blood
under my finger nails,
like you under my skin,
obstinate.

I have been
scouring these hands
for weeks. The blood
was gone in minutes
but some things
can't be removed by water,
or soap, or bleach,
or tears.

Some stains
can only fade
in the presence
of mercy and forgiveness.
Mercy from you,
forgiveness
from myself.

Crumbling

I convince myself
of my superiority
only to distract
me from my envy.
You tell me
we're all humans.
I tell you
some of us are better at it.
As I reach forward
to adjust your tie,
you just sigh.

These eyes,
that struggle
to locate
my contacts lenses
in the morning
without glasses,
can see your imperfections
immediately.

It is so much easier
to point out the fact that you
are crumbling,
than to accept that I
am already crumb.
So much more bearable
to point out your
flaws than it is
to acknowledge
my ceilings.

Shadow Of The Day

I had so much to say to you,
now all I can manage is
goodbye.

You were more than enough,
you built people from dust
and we will do you proud
got jammed at the lump
in my throat.

I am not the only one.
Cards and flowers
talk of royalty
and majesty,
but the ink is already
bleeding, the flowers
will wilt and you will
never know.

Acid tears sizzle
on the earth
as they land,
whilst wolves whine
like they are mourning
the final sunset.

Numb

I have walked across hot coals
all my life. They don't
burn the same as they used to.

Dealing with death
virtually as long as
I have been dodging
it, and death doesn't
hurt like it did before

I lost you.
I am numb.

On the surface
I look like I always did,
somewhere in the
undertow lives
a darkness that death
cannot compete with,
I can't escape from it.

I have walked across hot coals
all my life. Now
every step that I take scorches
the earth below my feet.

These feet, once scarred
by elevated temperatures,
do not ache anymore,
I sent my feeling away
with you.

Only you deserve it.

Forever

2 lighters
10 pounds
A packet of chewing gum
Her headphones

If you had asked her yesterday morning
this would have been the list of things
that she had lost this week. Now she sits

in the living room that you proposed
to her in and watches the news. She is
crying and trying not to recognise
your face through the tear varnish
that coats her bloodshot eyes.

She recalls watching news bulletins
like this with you, *young boy stabbed
in Hockley, father shot in Aston.*
The dead men of Birmingham.

She wonders now if someone is sitting
in their living room thanking God
that she has suffered this loss
rather than them. She understands,

above all else, she understands this feeling.
She holds a photo of you, with your
handwriting scratched across the back
in slightly smudged red ink.

Forever.

Casey Introduces...
Hannah Swings

Is a noun, not a verb. She is a writer, a visual artist and a teacher. She is a student of the Masters in Creative Writing at UoB, whose poetry will grace the stages of CUPSI 2018 in Philadelphia. Hannah Swings is someone who I consider to be a great friend and a greater artist. When we met a couple of years ago I was astounded by two things, the first was the quality of Hannah's poetry, the second was the fact that she wouldn't give herself credit for how good it was. I have taken a personal interest in Hannah's journey as a writer and imposed myself into her life as a friend. We have shared stages, shared coffees, shared pain, shared mini pancakes covered in chocolate sauce and strawberries, and now it is a privilege for me to share her with you. Her poem 'Freddie Mercury' is one that I fell in love with when I first heard it, and one I fall in love with again and again.

Freddie Mercury

When I am nine, my parents move us to the countryside, away
from bus routes and gang wars. The house they buy is bigger,
too cheap for what it offers and their deliberation doesn't last
long. They don't think to look at the old wiring; block out the
sound of the motorway at the bottom of the garden.
Financial recklessness is hereditary.

We continue to go to school in the city, work in the city: be city
dwellers that must sleep where we can see the stars clearer.
Thirteen miles there, another thirteen back: the car becomes
our living room, our bedroom, our home.
It doesn't have a CD player, so my brother makes jukebox
cassettes, one song per family member then repeat. I choose
Jesus of Surburbia by Green Day because it is nine minutes
and seven seconds long and I crave the attention.

Fields, trees, abandoned farm buildings, hair pin bends, blind
junctions, I know the landscape better than the opening to my
favourite movie.
I write birthday cards leaning on headrests without curving a
line.
I can apply a full face of makeup using the rear view mirror
from the backseat.
I learn to change outfits without flashing the driver.
I devour books like they will be burnt at the end of the day.

My brother falls in love with a girl who lives opposite our
school. He stays overnight on a camp bed in her living room, I
think. He stops making mixtapes.

I am given an ipod for my birthday and spend the mornings staring out of the window pretending I am in a music video.

My mother only drives when my Dad is already home. At night, she turns the lights off on roads without cat eyes and we scream in the seconds of darkness, before we flash back to visibility. One night, we drive passed a man in drag walking in the road towards us. Two weeks later, the local headlines talk of a "decapitated tranny" who got hit by a car on her way home from a dinner party.
My Mom stops turning the lights off after that.

Mornings mean minus six degrees and the heater breaks.

I fall in love with a boy who lives opposite my school in an adjacent road to my brother's girlfriend. I can see my art room from his bedroom window. I stay overnight on a camp bed, sometimes.
I'm not sure whether the reason I love him is because I get an extra half an hour of sleep in the morning.

We resurrect Freddie Mercury on a thunder filled October night through dramatic, unrehearsed yet surprisingly harmonised word-perfect rendition of Bohemian Rhapsody. We congratulate each other on hitting the high notes, swerve to miss a pheasant and hit a tree instead.

When I graduate - after thirteen years of thirteen miles there and thirteen back -my parents move to the road my brother's now fiancée lives on. I can see my art room from my bedroom window.

I get an extra half an hour of sleep in the morning.

There are bus routes and gang wars and no blind junctions.

We do not make mixtapes.

We do not resurrect Freddie Mercury anymore, but I can still apply liquid eyeliner travelling over potholes using the rear view mirror from the backseat.

Casey Introduces...
Sophie Wheeler

Sophie Wheeler is one of my students, and has been since she was 12 and I was younger than I am now! Now 16, Sophie has shown herself to be a number of things; a wonderful human, a talented young woman and a writer with more potential than she can ever comprehend. I told Sophie last year that her poetry would be published - she didn't know then that I had a plan. I am confident that one day she will have her own book; if I am fortunate I will be mentioned in the acknowledgements, if you are clever, you'll buy a copy. The poem she has contributed to this book, displays the developing talent of a young writer, and the unquantifiable vulnerability of a young heart.

Proud Of Me?

Dear Dad,
Apparently, I'm just like you.
From the way I speak,
To the things I do.
Everyone says how were just the same,
Even though I only know your name.
A missing part of my family tree
Daddy, are you proud of me?

19th of January 2003.
That dreaded day,
Engraved on me.
A mum and daughter left in pain.
You left when the angels came.
Leaving a broken family.
But tell me, Daddy, are you proud of me?

All the doctors could say was sorry,
As if it could bring back my daddy for mommy.
Taken with a bleeding brain,
Leaving two bleeding hearts,
Screaming out in pain.
You were gone and now ill never see,
If Daddy, are you proud of me?

A young girl, growing up,
So many questions on my mind.
About who you were, where you went,
And how we intertwined.
Why him? Why us? I'd ask my mom
And although she didn't know,
Shed tell me you were needed up there,
Which is why you had to go.
A little girl, so many questions,
Sitting on her mommy's knee.
And though even no answer would ever come,
She'd say, Daddy, are you proud of me?

But now I'm growing up,
And I speak to you through our stars,
I think of you as part of me,
And I'm proud of who we are.
Two broken hearts so far apart,
And yet we are so near.
You live on inside of me,
So, I know you're always here.
Though some things go, and others change,
What happens is meant to be.
But if there's one thing that I hope,
Its that Daddy, you'll be proud of me.

Casey Introduces...
Reuben Field

... is a Brummie, born, bred and proud. This is just one of the things that we have in common. Rueben is passionate about poetry and about education, and through many platforms he uses his words to enhance and enrich the lives of those he comes into contact with. As the winner of the Birmingham heat of BBC Radio 1xtra's Words First; the quality of Reuben's work has been recognised by many, and it is a privileged for me to introduce it to a new audience.

will be our next destination

Wherever trains stopped, the views were still blurred
deep burnt crimsons of rust on sullen dirt.
Teaming noises differed only in source,
amalgamated, constant, torn and coarse,
My lips bitter, bleeding, spitting and curt.

On disembarking, I would always curse,
yearned only for intoxicating turns
and folds of ultra slims round potent scores,
            wherever trains stopped.

Aimless, craving distance, home and to spurn,
I could not read road signs, would disjoint words.
I stumbled, always, whichever my course,
all purpose removed, all ambition paused.
Constant, desolate, the views were still blurred
            wherever trains stopped.

THANKYOU

Kerri Bailey, in a year where we became parents, and I had a million and one other things going on, you would have been well within your rights to put your foot down and tell me to push this book back, instead you did what you always did; you supported me and held me together.

Amerah Saleh, you are a constant inspiration and you always support and encourage me to push further, work harder and keep experimenting. Even when we drove for an hour, to find out that Kenilworth Castle was closed, you kept our spirits up, and we kept grafting.

Stuart Bartholomew, you believed in me and you challenged me just when I needed it most. What you are doing and will do at Verve is amazing and I will be supporting it all the way.

Raymond Antrobus, for asking me the questions that I needed somebody to ask me and for being the answer to so many questions.

Anne Holloway, you supported me in the release of *Waiting At Bloomsbury Park*, and after that you have continued to be a constant source of guidance and advice. I will forever be indebted to you and to Big White Shed.

ABOUT VERVE POETRY PRESS

Verve Poetry Press is a new press focussing initially on meeting a local need in Birmingham - a need for the vibrant poetry scene here in Brum to find a way to present itself to the poetry world via publication. Co-founded by Stuart Bartholomew and Amerah Saleh, it will be publishing poets this year from all corners of the city - poets that represent the city's varied and energetic qualities and will communicate its many poetic stories.

As well as this wonderful collection from Casey - look out in 2018 for stunning first collections from Amerah, Leon Priestnall, Nafeesa Hamid and Hannah Swings, to name but a few. And watch this new press bring the colour and attitude of Verve Poetry Festival, our sister in Birmingham based poetry activity, to all its publishing and event-making.

Like the festival, we will strive to think about poetry in inclusive ways and embrace the multiplicity of approaches towards this glorious art.

So watch this space. Verve Poetry Press has arrived.

www.vervepoetrypress.com
@VervePoetryPres
mail@vervepoetrypress.com